CPS-MORRILL ES

3 24571 0900729 8   920 GIF
10 kings & queens who changed

W9-ATF-076

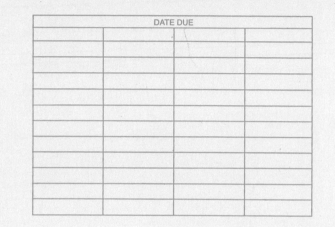

DATE DUE

920
GIF

3 24571 0900729 8
Gifford, Clive.

10 kings & queens
who changed the
world

MORRILL ES
CHICAGO PUBLIC SCHOOLS
6011 S ROCKWELL ST
CHICAGO, IL 60629

398239 01047   23588B   0001

Copyright © 2009 by Macmillan Children's Books
Additional illustrations by Sarah Cousens

KINGFISHER
Published in the United States by Kingfisher, an imprint of Henry
Holt and Company LLC, 175 Fifth Avenue, New York, New York 10010.
First published in Great Britain by Kingfisher Publications plc, an
imprint of Macmillan Children's Books, London.
All rights reserved
Distributed in Canada by H. B. Fenn and Company Ltd.

Library of Congress Cataloging-in-Publication Data
has been applied for.

ISBN: 978-0-7534-6252-2

Kingfisher books are available for special promotions and premiums.
For details contact: Director of Special Markets, Holtzbrinck Publishers.

First American Edition May 2009
Printed in Singapore
10 9 8 7 6 5 4 3 2 1
1TR/1208/TWP/MAR/150MA/C

Louis XIV
of France

Charles V, Holy
Roman Emperor

10
KINGS & QUEENS
WHO CHANGED THE WORLD

Written by Clive Gifford
Illustrated by David Cousens

KINGFISHER
NEW YORK

Pharaoh
Hatshepsut

Contents

Hatshepsut

For the ancient Egyptians who lived 3,500 years ago, it must have been an astonishing spectacle. A fleet of boats made of wood and papyrus reeds had just docked in Thebes, the capital city of the mighty Egyptian civilization. To mounting excitement, sailors unloaded great treasures from the expedition to the mysterious land of Punt, far to the south of Egypt's empire.

The crowd looked on in wonder as the strange cargoes were taken into Thebes to be weighed and cataloged: clay jars full of incense and spices; living myrrh trees; gold, silver, ivory, and ebony; baboons, giraffes, and other astonishing animals. All eyes turned to Egypt's leader, the pharaoh Hatshepsut. For although she claimed that her dead father and the gods had ordered the expedition, it had been her plan—and hers alone.

Hatshepsut's ships might have been transported across the desert before they sailed south to the coast of Punt.

As the pharaoh, Hatshepsut wore a double crown on ceremonial occasions. It featured the white crown of Upper Egypt and the red crown of Lower Egypt joined together.

As a member of the royal family, Hatshepsut had a privileged upbringing under the watchful eye of her nanny, Sitre.

Hatshepsut was one of the first great queens. She reigned during the 18th dynasty of ancient Egypt (1550–1282 B.C.), when this extraordinary civilization was at its peak of wealth and power. Hatshepsut was the daughter of Pharaoh Thutmose I. She married Thutmose II, her half brother, who became pharaoh after the death of Thutmose I.

Queen Hatshepsut had a daughter but no male heir. Thutmose II had a son by a different wife. When Thutmose II died, his son (Thutmose III) was too young to become pharaoh. A crisis threatened the empire. As the senior member of the royal family and Thutmose III's stepmother, Hatshepsut was appointed regent (a form of coruler), while priests and officials were most likely in charge of running Egypt. Hatshepsut might have had a role in the government, but she wanted more power.

Gradually, Hatshepsut took the daring steps toward becoming pharaoh of Egypt. Women in ancient Egypt could own land and inherit wealth, but a queen declaring herself the pharaoh was extremely rare. Hatshepsut had a fight on her hands to keep ahold of power.

Hatshepsut had huge obelisks erected at the massive temple complex in Karnak, outside Thebes. These giant stone pillars were cut from single pieces of rock in Aswan and ferried by barge up the Nile River.

Hatshepsut was a quick-witted ruler. To stay in favor with powerful priests and to link her more closely with the gods, she improved many of Egypt's temples. She used propaganda to emphasize her royal blood. She even wore the clothing and false beard of a male pharaoh and gave up titles that could be held only by a woman.

During her reign of 22 years, Hatshepsut ruled jointly with Thutmose III, but there is little doubt that she was completely in charge. She kept Thutmose busy in the army as it marched south into Upper Egypt and Nubia and voyaged to the land of Punt. The glorious success of this expedition helped strengthen Hatshepsut's grip on power.

The pharaoh surrounded herself with skilled viziers (advisers), chief among them being Senemut. Originally the tutor of Hatshepsut's daughter, Senemut rose up the ranks and gained more than 40 titles. As the pharaoh's chief architect, Senemut designed the awe-inspiring mortuary temple in Deir el-Bahri, the grandest of the many construction projects completed during Hatshepsut's reign.

Pharaoh Hatshepsut began to wear male clothing such as the nemes headdress, khat head cloth, shendyt kilt, and a ceremonial false beard.

Hatshepsut's magnificent temple in Deir el-Bahri was partly cut out of solid rock. Its walls and pillars were decorated with scenes from her reign.

Hatshepsut's name, in an oval cartouche, was found on jewelry and carved onto walls.

Hatshepsut's army, led by Thutmose III (far left), marched south to Nubia to quell a rebellion at least once during her reign.

What we know about Hatshepsut comes from court records, histories written long after her death, and archaeological evidence. Her tomb was found in 1903, but it took more than 100 years to identify her mummy. Many mysteries are still to be solved. Hatshepsut's reign ended abruptly in around 1458 B.C. Was she murdered, did she die peacefully, or did she simply retire from ruling? What is certain is that Hatshepsut was a legendary ruler and a queen who dared to become the pharaoh.

Mysteriously, many statues of Hatshepsut were destroyed after her reign. Her name and cartouche were often replaced with those of Thutmose III.

LIFE LINK
Hatshepsut claimed a divine right to rule Egypt, handed down to her by the god Amen-Ra. Around 1,100 years later, Alexander the Great marched into Egypt and was crowned pharaoh. He was hailed by Egyptian priests as the son of the king of the gods, Amen.

Alexander the Great

Around 344 B.C. Alexander of Macedon, the son of King Philip II, eyed a beautiful wild horse, brought to his father's court by a trader. Alexander, not yet a teenager, defied his father by claiming that he could tame the powerful animal. Noticing that the horse was disturbed by the movement of its own shadow, he guided it to face directly into the sun, gained its trust . . . and leaped onto its back. An anxious crowd watched the boy master his mount, which he named Bucephalus.

Philip II had already made Macedon a powerful kingdom. Now he was conquering the warring states of Greece to the south. Alexander grew up in a country almost permanently at war and learned military tactics and martial arts from his tutor.

After Bucephalus was tamed by Alexander, the two became inseparable for 18 years. The horse eventually died from wounds received in Alexander's last great battle.

Alexander's army burned the Greek city of Thebes to the ground. Around 6,000 Thebans were killed and thousands more were sold into slavery.

Philip II was planning to attack the Persians when he was murdered at his daughter's wedding in 336 B.C. The Macedon army accepted the 20-year-old Alexander as their new king. He showed a ruthless streak at once, executing nobles who were a potential threat. Some Greek cities were planning to revolt, but in 335 B.C., Alexander marched on the city of Thebes. His assault was so ferocious that the other Greek states were cowed into submission.

The famous Greek philosopher and scientist Aristotle was Alexander's tutor. He gave Alexander a copy of Homer's *Iliad*, an epic poem about the Trojan War, which Alexander kept with him throughout his military campaigns.

With opposition crushed in Greece, Alexander turned his attention to the Persian Empire in the east, ruled by King Darius III. He drew together a large force of around 35,000 men from peoples throughout Greece. Alongside the soldiers were engineers, architects, court officials, and servants. As many as 50,000 other Greeks became mercenaries in the Persian armies that fought against Alexander.

Alexander's troops marched eastward into the region that is now Turkey, defeating the forces of the Persian satraps (governors) and conquering hill tribes and small cities. Finally, they encountered a gigantic Persian army on a narrow plain in Issus.

Alexander was a brave and cunning military tactician. His army completely crushed the enemy, captured Darius III's wife, mother, and daughters, and forced the king himself to flee. Darius asked Alexander to surrender and to return his family. The request was met with these chilling words: "Do not write to me as to an equal. Everything you possess is now mine . . . Wherever you may hide, be sure I shall seek you out."

Two years would pass before the kings faced each other in battle again. During that time, Alexander won control of the eastern coastline of the Mediterranean Sea. He knew that he could not defeat the mighty Persian fleet that controlled the sea, but he could make it powerless by conquering the ports that supplied the ships. Sidon and Byblos fell quickly and Damascus was taken. The city of Tyre held out for seven months before Alexander finally gained control.

Alexander pressed on to Egypt, which fell with only a few skirmishes. He was even crowned pharaoh in 332 B.C. but was soon on the move once again.

Alexander began his siege of Tyre by building a stone causeway, complete with siege towers, toward the island city. Defenders fought back fiercely, showing Alexander that he would need a navy in order to take Tyre.

Alexander's foot soldiers fought in a tightly packed unit called a phalanx. Armed with 13-ft. (4-m)-long sarissa spears, they kept the enemy in place while the cavalry attacked from the side and rear.

Alexander's view that he had a divine right to conquer and rule was reinforced when he visited the oracle of Amen in Egypt. There he was hailed by a priest as the son of Amen, the king of the gods.

In Gaugamela, Alexander (far right) charged through a gap in the Persian ranks. He reached Darius's chariot and killed its driver. Darius managed to escape and fled into the mountains.

In 331 B.C., the forces of Darius and Alexander clashed again in Gaugamela in Babylonia. Darius had rebuilt his army, now equipped with Indian elephants, chariots with sharp blades protruding from their wheel axles, and vicious metal spikes called caltrops.

All this would be of no use—Alexander triumphed again. Darius fled and tried to build a third army, only to be murdered by his own men. Alexander marched deep into Persia, capturing the wealthy cities of Babylon and Susa, as well as the ultimate prize of Persepolis—the capital of the empire and the site of the magnificent palace of Xerxes. But he stayed for only four months before burning down the palace, most likely in a drunken rage.

The Persian wealth taken by Alexander was extraordinary. It is believed that it took 20,000 mules and 4,000 camels to transport all the gold, silver, and jewels. Alexander had much of it melted down and turned into coins to pay his armies.

Alexander was clever and forward thinking—he built more than 60 new cities throughout his empire, which stretched across parts of three continents. He was often generous to his friends but also had a devastating temper. He ordered the killing of his general Parmenio in 330 B.C., murdered his friend Cleitus two years later, and executed many of his governors. He argued with his own people, who did not like him adopting Persian clothes and customs or styling himself as a king descended directly from the gods.

At the Battle of Hydaspes, the army of King Porus used fighting elephants— powerful and terrifying opponents for the exhausted Macedonian troops.

Alexander continued to march through Asia, crossing the Indus River and defeating the Indian king, Porus, at the Battle of Hydaspes. By the autumn of 326 B.C., the king remained unbeaten, but his exhausted troops wanted to go home. He finally agreed to their wishes but insisted on dividing the armies into three groups for the trip. Alexander's own group suffered terribly from lack of food and water as they passed through treacherous deserts.

Alexander showed support for his troops by refusing extra water rations.

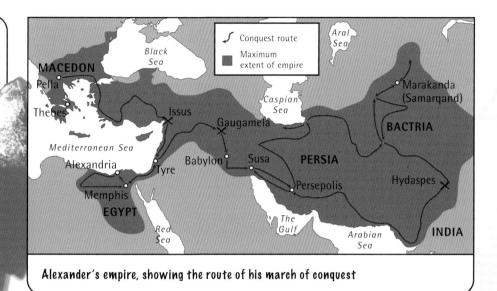

Alexander's empire, showing the route of his march of conquest

In Babylon in the spring of 323 B.C., Alexander began to plan further conquests, but he fell gravely ill. No one knows whether he was a victim of poisoning or had contracted malaria or another illness. He died in June at the age of only 32. It was unclear who would succeed Alexander as king, and his empire suffered more than 40 years of infighting before three separate realms emerged.

In only 13 years, Alexander created the greatest empire that the world had ever seen. By building new cities and encouraging Greeks to settle in his conquered lands, Alexander helped usher in the Hellenistic period—an era lasting almost 300 years that saw Greek language, culture, and influence spread across large parts of Europe, North Africa, and western Asia.

Hephaestion was Alexander's second in command and his closest friend. The king grieved uncontrollably at Hephaestion's death in 324 B.C. and lay with the body for many hours.

LIFE LINK
Both Alexander and Charlemagne built on their fathers' successes to develop their kingdoms into mighty empires, relying on fast-moving cavalry forces to win battles. Within 50 years of both conquerors' deaths, their empires were split into three parts.

Charlemagne

September A.D. 768. King Pepin the Short, the leader of the Frankish tribes, lay dying. As was the custom, Pepin divided his territory between his sons. Carloman was given the eastern lands; his older brother, Charlemagne, received the western territories. Three years later, Carloman died, leaving Charlemagne as the leader of Europe's largest kingdom.

Einhard, a monk at Charlemagne's royal court in Aachen (now in Germany), described the king as "strong and noble in height, measuring seven times his own foot." The king towered over his countrymen, but in other ways he chose not to stand out. He did not like rowdy or drunken behavior and wore the typical linen tunic and breeches (pants) of the Franks.

In order to eliminate the traditional religion and rituals of the Saxon people, Charlemagne ordered the destruction of many of their sacred sites.

In 772, Charlemagne led his troops out of France to invade the region that is now the Netherlands and Germany. He defeated the Lombards of northern Italy and declared himself their king in 774. He began a 32-year conflict with the Saxons to the east, and in the 790s, he drove deep into Central and Eastern Europe to conquer the Avars of Hungary.

Charlemagne's armies were skilled and well organized. He sent out spies and scouts, split his forces into two groups to confuse the enemy, and deployed a highly mobile cavalry, armed with long swords, ahead of massed ranks of infantry. Charlemagne could be merciful to his prisoners, but in 782, he ordered the execution of 4,500 Saxons in a single day.

Charlemagne's grand coronation took place at St. Peter's Basilica in Rome. The title of *Holy Roman Emperor* survived for more than 1,000 years, until 1806.

Charlemagne often led his fierce Frankish warriors into battle armed with a long, heavy sword called *Joyeuse*, meaning "joyful."

Charlemagne was a Christian, and he tried to convert the pagan peoples he conquered. During a visit to Rome, he came to the aid of Pope Leo III, who had been attacked by a gang that tried to cut off his tongue and gouge out his eyes. Leo returned the favor by crowning Charlemagne the Holy emperor of all Romans on Christmas, 800.

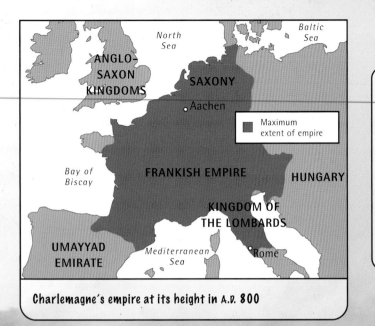

North Sea

Baltic Sea

ANGLO-SAXON KINGDOMS

SAXONY

• Aachen

FRANKISH EMPIRE

HUNGARY

Bay of Biscay

KINGDOM OF THE LOMBARDS

UMAYYAD EMIRATE

Mediterranean Sea

• Rome

Maximum extent of empire

Charlemagne's empire at its height in A.D. 800

The Palatine Chapel stood at the heart of Charlemagne's palace. Scholars, architects, and philosophers traveled to the court, and Aachen became a great center of learning.

Charlemagne was not only a warrior. He worked hard to bring order to his sometimes wild and lawless lands and made reforms to the church. He created a new system of coins based on a standard weight of silver and tried to improve justice across his empire.

Although barely educated as a child, Charlemagne was quick-witted and good with numbers. He set up a library at his court and employed famous scholars to teach him. Charlemagne could not write, but he learned to speak Greek and Latin and had books read aloud to him. To revive the arts, he brought great painters, sculptors, and musicians from Rome to Aachen.

Charlemagne tried to build a giant canal to link the Danube and Rhine rivers. His ambitious plan was defeated by bad weather and soggy ground.

Charlemagne was a masterful war tactician who would tell his nobles exactly how many soldiers he needed for each expedition.

In 792, Charlemagne thwarted a plot against him involving his eldest son, Pepin the Hunchback. The other rebels were executed, while Pepin was disowned and banished to a monastery for life. It was the last real threat to Charlemagne's power, despite attacks in the 800s from the Danes and Vikings to the north and the Saracens to the south. His empire was made up of many different, and sometimes warring, peoples. It was proof of his skill that he was able to keep it intact.

Before his death in 814, Charlemagne had planned to divide the empire among his three remaining sons, all born to Hildegard, the second of his four wives. Two, however, died within one year of each other, leaving only Louis the Pious to succeed Charlemagne as emperor. After the death of Louis in 840, the lands were divided into a number of territories.

In less than 30 years, Charlemagne's empire had crumbled, but his reputation would grow for centuries. He had created the foundations of powerful future nations such as France and Germany, and he became a model for European warrior kings to come. To some, he was remembered by the Latin title given to him by one of his court poets—*rex pater Europae*, or King Father of Europe.

Charlemagne was a great warrior, but in 778, his army suffered its worst defeat at the hands of the Basques of northern Spain.

LIFE LINK
In 800, Charlemagne was crowned the first Holy Roman Emperor. More than 700 years later, King Henry VIII of England clashed with the Holy Roman Emperor at the time, Charles V, over his demand for a divorce from Charles's aunt, Catherine of Aragon.

Henry VIII

November 1501. Ten-year-old Henry Tudor led the lavish wedding procession of his elder brother, Arthur, through London to St. Paul's Cathedral. Their father, King Henry VII, had carefully built up England's finances but now spared no expense on the celebrations. Yet, less than four months later, Arthur lay dead from a mystery illness. An agreement was struck that when Henry was older, he would marry his brother's wife, Catherine of Aragon.

Henry married Catherine in 1509. Within weeks, he was the king. England rejoiced at the crowning of its new ruler after years of his father's high taxes. Tall, intelligent, and handsome, Henry was many people's idea of the perfect king. But he was also a gambler—according to one ambassador, he would often wager the huge sum of up to 8,000 ducats (gold coins) in a single day.

Henry loved to play real tennis, an early racket sport that was played on an indoor court. He was also an avid hunter, archer, and dancer.

The *Henri Grâce à Dieu* was launched in 1514. Armed with 43 heavy cannon and another 141 guns, it was Europe's largest and most powerful warship.

Henry had a sharp mind and a temper to match. He was pampered as a boy, and it is said that he even had a whipping boy, a companion who was punished every time Henry misbehaved.

Henry set out to enjoy himself as a king with almost limitless energy. Artists and musicians flocked to his court; he threw lavish banquets and tournaments; and he excelled in hunts, often riding half a dozen horses to exhaustion. Henry spent a fortune building up his navy to more than 50 ships, including enormous fighting vessels such as the *Mary Rose* and the *Henri Grâce à Dieu*.

Henry longed for military success. In 1513, his troops marched into French territory and also defeated the hostile Scots in Flodden, killing their king, James IV.

The man in charge of Henry's French forces was Thomas Wolsey. In 1515, he completed a rapid rise to power by taking control of the church in England, as well as governing Henry's kingdom on day-to-day matters. For the next ten years, Wolsey was England's most powerful and wealthy man after the king. Wolsey even built a palace in Hampton Court that outshone any of Henry's homes. While the king sometimes pressed for war, Wolsey concentrated on keeping the peace between England and the three great European powers of France, Spain, and the Holy Roman Empire.

Henry's forces captured Tournai in 1513. Five years later, they handed the city back to France.

In 1520, Henry held peace talks with Francis I of France. The meeting was so extravagant that it became known as the Field of the Cloth of Gold.

Henry's marriage to Catherine was filled with tragedies. Only one of their six children, Mary, survived beyond infancy. The king feared that he would never have a male heir to his throne. He fell in love with Anne Boleyn in 1525, and from then on his main concern, or "great matter," was to find a way to divorce Catherine and marry Anne. Henry argued that his marriage to his brother's widow went against God, and he sent Wolsey to Rome to ask Pope Clement VII to grant a divorce. But the pope, swayed by Catherine's nephew, Charles V, refused.

Henry was so furious with Thomas Wolsey that he seized Hampton Court palace. Wolsey died in 1530 before he could be executed on charges of treason.

In a rage, Henry replaced Wolsey with Thomas More as the lord chancellor and promoted Thomas Cromwell and Thomas Cranmer to powerful positions. As the archbishop of Canterbury, in 1533, Cranmer declared Henry's marriage to Catherine illegal, by which time Henry had already married Anne Boleyn in secret.

Now Henry set off a chain of events that would change religion in England forever. He broke away from the Roman Catholic church and the pope's control, declaring himself the supreme head of the Church of England. Many Catholics had to choose between his authority or the pope's. Those who refused to swear an oath to Henry, including Thomas More and some Catholics throughout England (there was a major revolt in the north in 1536–1537), were arrested and executed.

Henry's soldiers ransacked churches for their valuable treasures, while church land was sold to nobles at bargain prices. A handful of monks and nuns who resisted were sent to prison or executed.

Henry had spent most of the money that had been so painstakingly saved by his father, so he dissolved (closed) abbeys, monasteries, and convents and sold church possessions and lands. Still longing for a son, he became tired of Anne Boleyn and had her executed on charges of adultery. Within 11 days, he had married one of Anne's ladies in waiting, Jane Seymour. She finally gave the king a son, Edward, in 1537. But the new queen never recovered from a difficult birth— 12 days later, she died.

Anne Boleyn was beheaded at the Tower of London in 1536. Just three years earlier she had sailed down the River Thames in a fleet of 300 barges to be crowned queen.

During a joust in 1536, Henry was unseated by his opponent. The armored horse fell on top of the king, who lay unconscious for two hours.

In 1536, Henry suffered a leg wound while jousting. Due to the inflammation of the ulcer and the effects of aging, the king's weight greatly increased. His waist expanded to almost 55 in. (140cm), he had to walk using a cane, and he suffered from boils all over his body. Henry became unpredictable, paranoid, and prone to fits of rage, which led to the executions of many of his trusted advisers and nobles.

Thomas Cromwell tried to forge an alliance between England and Europe's non-Catholic powers by arranging Henry's wedding to a German noblewoman, Anne of Cleves. The pair got divorced quickly, and Cromwell paid for the mistake with his life on the same day in 1540 that Henry married his fifth wife, the beautiful Catherine Howard. There was a 30-year age difference between the two, and the queen unwisely had extramarital affairs. Henry found out, and in 1542, she was beheaded. The following year, Henry married his sixth and final wife, Catherine Parr.

Henry ordered the destruction of an entire village in order to build the grand Nonsuch Palace. By the end of his reign, the king owned an incredible 55 palaces.

Fearing an invasion by Europe's Catholic nations, Henry built a string of fortresses along England's coast in the 1540s.

Henry chose his fourth wife by studying five portraits. He was turned down by Christina of Milan (left) but accepted by Anne of Cleves (right).

Henry suffered great pain as he grew older. His ulcer had to be drained of infected fluids daily.

From 1542 to 1544, Henry tried to recapture his youthful vigor and some of England's glory by waging wars against Scotland and France. His armies achieved little but cost a fortune, almost bankrupting England. In 1546, the king fell seriously ill, and he died the following year.

As a truly larger-than-life figure, Henry is remembered for his extravagance and overspending, his six wives, and his terrible temper. But he also improved England's defenses and navy and created something revolutionary in Europe at the time—a country in which the king and state had authority over the church.

LIFE LINK

In 1520, Henry VIII's first wife, Catherine of Aragon, urged her nephew, Charles V, to make an alliance with the English king. More than 30 years later, in 1554, Henry's daughter, Mary, married Charles's son, Philip II.

Charles V

October 1555. A 55-year-old man, too sick to ride a horse, arrived on a small mule at the Ducal Palace in Brussels. In the packed Parliament Hall, many of the crowd wept as he gave an extraordinary speech, handing over his huge empire to his son and his brother. The speaker was Charles V, the Holy Roman Emperor, also known as Charles I of Spain.

Charles was born in Ghent (now in Belgium). When he was only three years old, his parents left for Spain. There, they lived at the court of Charles's grandparents, King Ferdinand II of Aragon and Queen Isabella of Castile, whose marriage had united most of Spain.

Charles, dressed all in black, ended his emotional resignation speech with these words: "If there be any here whom I have wronged, believe it was not intended and grant me their forgiveness."

Charles's mother, Joanna, was the heir to the Spanish kingdoms, but she never got the chance to reign. Overcome with grief at the death of her husband in 1506 and betrayed by others, she was kept under guard at the castle at Tordesillas on the orders of her father.

Charles was brought up in the Netherlands by his aunt, Margaret of Hapsburg. As a child, he developed a deep respect for the Roman Catholic church.

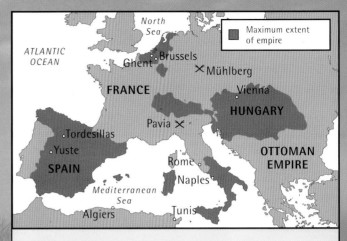

The extent of Charles's empire in Europe in 1520

Guillaume de Croy (on horseback) was a nobleman who became Charles's main tutor in 1509. It was de Croy who inspired Charles's love of chivalry, the code of honor adopted by knights.

When Charles reached Spain in 1517, he had not seen his mother for 14 years. Following the death of her husband, she traveled around Spain with his coffin and was nicknamed Joanna the Mad.

The young Charles was fascinated by knights and chivalry. He was much less interested in politics, but his position and family connections meant that the topic could not be avoided. After his father's death, Charles became the duke of Burgundy at the tender age of six. Even though he was not fully in power, Charles was expected to award knighthoods and carry out many other duties.

In 1516, Ferdinand II died. As his grandson and heir, Charles set sail for Spain in a fleet of 40 ships. Little did he know that within three years he would rule the largest empire in Europe since ancient Roman times.

In 1520, Charles visited his aunt, Catherine of Aragon, who was married to King Henry VIII. The two kings formed a brief alliance against France.

The Revolt of the Comuneros was a rebellion against Charles's reign that began with a public uprising in Toledo, Spain. After crushing the rebels, Charles signed more than 270 death warrants.

Charles arrived in Spain with some people questioning his right to rule. He spoke French and Flemish but not Spanish, and his appearance was far from inspiring. He was slightly built, with bulging eyes, a large nose, and an oversize lower jaw. But he moved quickly to secure the kingship. He was crowned Charles I—the first single monarch of Spain—and appointed many of his advisers from northern Europe as governors.

In 1519, Charles also became the ruler of the Hapsburg lands of central Europe following the death of his other grandfather, Maximilian I. He then bribed important officials to elect him as Holy Roman Emperor. One year later, he was crowned king of Germany.

Charles is said to have boasted that "the sun never sets in my realm." The territory he ruled over was vast, but with it came equally large problems. Charles spent much of his life fighting enemies from both outside and within his empire. In 1520, Spanish nobles stirred up a rebellion against Charles's governors called the Revolt of the Comuneros. The king rushed back to Spain, defeating the rebels.

Charles's rival for the title of Holy Roman Emperor had been Francis I, the king of France, who soon attacked Charles's lands in Italy. The French were defeated in Pavia in 1525, in the first of many wars between the states. The next clash saw Francis join forces with Pope Clement VII and Henry VIII of England to drive Charles's armies out of Italy. They failed, and the emperor's unpaid troops rampaged through Rome, looting and burning churches.

During the Sack of Rome, Charles's soldiers destroyed or stole paintings, statues, and sacred objects. They even imprisoned the pope for seven months.

At the Battle of Pavia, Charles's troops thrashed the French armies and captured their king, Francis I (below). He was released only after signing a humiliating treaty.

Although Charles was shocked by the Sack of Rome, as the rampage became known, it worked in his favor. The pope had no choice but to agree to the king's demands, which included blocking the divorce of Henry VIII from Catherine of Aragon and granting his formal coronation as Charles V, the Holy Roman Emperor, in 1530.

Even though Charles had a slim build, he gorged himself at mealtimes, often awaking at 5 A.M. to feast and drink beer.

Charles was determined to build a global empire, but further threats to his lands diverted his attention. The Muslim forces of the Ottoman Empire, which controlled most of the Mediterranean Sea region, launched repeated attacks from the south and the east. Led by Suleiman the Magnificent, they invaded Hungary, tried to capture Vienna, and overtook Naples in Italy.

During Charles's reign, Spanish soldiers known as conquistadors defeated the Aztec and Inca civilizations in Central and South America.

As soon as Charles felt that he had one enemy under control, another would attack a different part of his empire. A third war with the French erupted in 1535, the same year that Charles's forces captured Tunis in North Africa from the Ottomans. He himself led a force to crush a revolt in his home city of Ghent in 1540, before embarking on a disastrous naval and land battle against the Ottomans in Algiers one year later. Continually at war, his empire's funds were shrinking and its debts mounting. Of his many territories, only Spain was largely at peace.

Charles was a brave soldier who often fought alongside his men, despite his importance. When one adviser rebuked him, Charles replied, "We are short of men, and I could not set a bad example."

Martin Luther was a German monk who objected to many aspects of the Roman Catholic church. In 1521, he established his own Lutheran church. Those who followed Luther became known as Protestants, because they "protested" their new faith against Catholicism.

After Charles had crushed the revolt in Ghent, he forced 50 citizens to walk the streets barefoot, dressed only in white shirts, each with a noose around their neck.

Meanwhile, a huge revolution against the Roman Catholic church had begun. It was called the Reformation. Nobles in Germany and elsewhere were part of this movement. Refusing to accept the power of the pope, they became Protestants. Charles insisted that there could be only one religion in his empire, and in 1547, he defeated a large Protestant army in Mühlberg. Five years later, however, he signed the Peace of Passau, which allowed some religious freedom to certain groups of Protestants.

By the mid-1550s, the empire was again at war with France. Charles was exhausted and severely ill. He had had enough. He began to give up his titles, passing them to his son, Philip, and his brother, Ferdinand. By 1556, Charles had retired to a monastery in Spain. There, two years later, the former commander of the largest empire of his era died, surrounded by priests reading him psalms.

LIFE LINK
Charles V spent almost 30 years trying to repel the Ottoman forces of Suleiman the Magnificent. He defended Vienna from invasion and sacked Suleiman's stronghold in Tunis but suffered heavy defeats in Algiers and at the Battle of Preveza.

At the monastery in Yuste, Charles turned his back on power. He devoted his life to prayer, reading, fishing, music, art, and his large collection of clocks.

Suleiman the Magnificent

December 1522. After 145 brutal, bloodthirsty days, the siege of the Mediterranean island of Rhodes was over. Monstrous cannon and mines had reduced parts of the walls to rubble. Thousands of Ottoman soldiers had stormed through the breaches; thousands more had been killed by the gallant but vastly outnumbered defenders, the Knights of St. John.

The young leader of the Ottomans, Suleiman I, had barely begun his reign, but already Europe knew of his strength. He had captured one of the best-defended places in the Christian world, but he also showed mercy by allowing the survivors to leave freely.

Ottoman janissaries—the elite troops of the empire—storm the walls of Rhodes. Despite being outnumbered 13 to one, the Christian knights held out for almost five months.

Suleiman was born in Trebizond (now Trabzon, Turkey) on the southern shore of the Black Sea. He was the only son of the fiery Selim I, who deposed his own father in 1512 to become the sultan (ruler) of the Ottoman Empire. From the age of 15, Suleiman was the *sancak beyi* (governor) of Kaffa and then Manisa. Selim reigned for only eight years, but he greatly extended the empire and exterminated many rivals in order to gain the throne. By the time Suleiman came to power in 1520, there were few threats to his rule inside the empire and his mighty army was ready to advance . . .

On hearing of his father's death, Suleiman rode quickly from Manisa to catch a ship to Konstantiniyye (now Istanbul), the capital of the Ottoman Empire.

As a young boy, Suleiman became close friends with Ibrahim (far left), a former slave. Ibrahim went on to become the second most powerful man in the empire.

Suleiman began to expand his empire in almost every direction. He conquered the city of Belgrade in 1521, captured Rhodes, and then advanced into Hungary in 1526 to defeat the armies of King Louis II at the Battle of Mohács. Hungary would be divided up and fought over by the Ottoman and Austrian empires for the next 300 years.

Three years after Mohács, Suleiman attacked Vienna, but the defenders of the Austrian city held out. A second siege in 1532 was thwarted by bad weather and lack of supplies, but by then Suleiman was firmly in control of a large part of eastern Europe.

In Mohács, the well-trained, musket-wielding Ottoman infantry slaughtered more than 14,000 Hungarian soldiers.

Suleiman's *tughra*, or official signature, was intricate and beautiful. Under his reign, the art of calligraphy flourished.

The Ottoman advances sent shock waves throughout Europe. Suleiman came into conflict with Charles V, the other great empire builder of the era. Charles tried to create an alliance of Christian countries, but Suleiman cleverly encouraged the Europeans to squabble among themselves, which prevented them from uniting against the Muslim Ottomans.

At the Battle of Preveza in 1538, Ottoman ships were outnumbered two to one but still destroyed 13 Christian vessels and captured 36 more.

The forces of Charles V and Suleiman clashed again and again for control of the Mediterranean Sea and North Africa. Charles captured Tunis in 1535; three years later, his ships joined forces with a Venetian fleet to take on the Ottoman navy at the Battle of Preveza. The Ottomans, led by the former pirate Khayr ad-Din, won a crushing victory that gave Suleiman control of many North African ports and much of the Mediterranean Sea for the next 30 years. Ottoman naval power also stretched to the Black and Red seas, and in 1538, Suleiman even sent a fleet to India to help the local ruler fight off Portuguese attacks.

Ottoman naval leader Khayr ad-Din was known as Barbarossa in the West. He terrorized enemy ships until the 1540s.

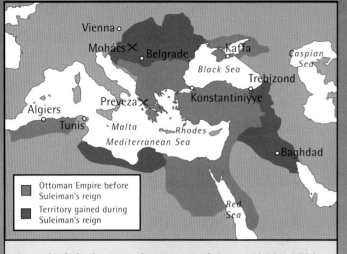

Growth of the Ottoman Empire under Suleiman, 1520-1566

In 1535, Suleiman and Ibrahim rode triumphantly into Baghdad. Faced by the fearsome Ottoman army, the commander of the city had surrendered without a fight.

In spite of more wars—including three campaigns against Persia between 1533 and 1554—the heart of the Ottoman Empire flourished. Suleiman ordered the construction of mosques, aqueducts, and *mekteb*s (schools) in Konstantiniyye and other towns. In 1539, he appointed Mimar Sinan as his head architect. Sinan alone oversaw the building of 25 libraries, 17 hospitals, and a remarkable 132 mosques, including the majestic Suleymaniye Mosque.

Suleiman inspired a great flowering in the Ottoman arts. A fine poet himself (in both the Turkish and Persian languages), he gave help and encouragement to artists, calligraphers, writers, metalworkers, and jewelers, the best of whom he gathered around him at his court.

Suleiman set up artistic societies known as *Ehl-i Hiref*—Communities of the Talented—throughout the Ottoman Empire.

One of Suleiman's greatest monuments is the Suleymaniye Mosque, with its 174-ft. (53-m)-high dome. The four giant towers, called minarets, each have ten balconies, signifying that Suleiman was the tenth sultan of the empire.

Known and feared as Suleiman the Magnificent throughout Europe, in his own lands he was given the name *Suleiman Kanuni*—the Lawgiver. He helped write new laws that made taxes and land ownership fairer. He demanded that his governors rule justly and honestly, although this was easier to achieve at the heart of the empire than farther away.

As the years passed, plots bubbled up at the Ottoman court. Suleiman's childhood friend Ibrahim had been appointed grand vizier in 1523. His rapid rise, lavish palace, and extravagant spending made him many enemies, including Suleiman's wife, Roxelana. No one knows who, if anyone, organized a plot or trap, but Ibrahim suddenly fell from favor. He was executed in 1536.

Roxelana might also have plotted to kill her stepson, Mustafa, so that her own sons could succeed Suleiman. Mustafa was executed in 1553 on suspicion of plotting to overthrow the sultan. Roxelana's sons, Selim and Bayezid, were put in charge of parts of the empire but began warring. Forced to choose between the two, Suleiman sent an army to help Selim defeat Bayezid.

Suleiman's wife, Roxelana, was a powerful figure at the Ottoman court. She had been brought to Konstantiniyye as a slave. Suleiman broke tradition by allowing her to accompany him at court throughout his life.

The year before his death, Suleiman's forces again besieged the Knights of St. John, now based in Malta. Despite huge losses over three months of bitter fighting, this time the knights held out. Suleiman ended his reign in 1566 almost as he had begun it, on the battlefields of Hungary. Transported by carriage all the way from Konstantiniyye, the sultan died two days before his forces claimed victory in Szigetvár. He had inherited a strong country from his father, but it was Suleiman's strength and intelligence that propelled the empire to the peak of its wealth, influence, and power.

Suleiman's government met at the dazzling Topkapi Palace in Konstantiniyye.

Suleiman's son, Mustafa, was executed in the traditional way, strangled with a string from an archer's bow.

LIFE LINK
Suleiman's siege of Malta greatly alarmed Elizabeth I. She feared that if the Knights of St. John were beaten, Europe would be at his mercy. She later sent gifts to the mother of Sultan Mehmed III, hoping that he would send Ottoman ships to help the English fight Spain.

Elizabeth I

September 1533. Elizabeth Tudor's birth was a great disappointment to her mother, Anne Boleyn, and her father, King Henry VIII. Both had desperately wanted a boy to be the heir to the throne of England.

Within three years, Elizabeth's mother was dead, executed on charges of adultery. In 1537, Henry's third wife, Jane Seymour, gave birth to a son, Edward. Both Elizabeth and her elder half-sister, Mary Tudor, lost their title of princess. Eventually, Elizabeth was taken under the wing of Henry's sixth and final wife, Catherine Parr.

Lady Jane Grey ruled England for nine days in 1553 before Mary Tudor took power. She was beheaded one year later.

In 1554, Thomas Wyatt plotted to overthrow Mary and make Elizabeth queen. Elizabeth was taken prisoner and held under threat of execution for eight weeks.

After Henry's death in 1547, Edward was crowned king, aged only nine. Behind the scenes, ambitious nobles jostled for control. Catherine Parr's new husband, Thomas Seymour, was accused of plotting to marry Elizabeth and seize the throne. He was executed in 1549, but Elizabeth survived a grueling interrogation. In 1553, Edward died and Mary Tudor was crowned queen. Elizabeth fell under suspicion again. She was imprisoned in the Tower of London while advisers to Queen Mary urged her execution.

By 1558, relations between the two half sisters had thawed. Mary, childless and dying, finally agreed to name Elizabeth as her heir. Mary had married Philip II, who became the king of Spain in 1556, and had tried to make England a Catholic nation once again. The crowning of Elizabeth, a Protestant, was greeted with great joy by many people. Their new queen was quick-witted and bright, but she had a sharp temper, too. At the age of only 25, she inherited a nation ravaged by poor harvests and unsuccessful wars, facing the danger of being torn apart by a religious uprising.

Queen Mary overturned her father's religious reforms, and almost 300 Protestants who refused to become Catholics were burned at the stake.

Elizabeth enjoyed Tudor sports and pastimes such as hunting and the cruel sport of bearbaiting. In 1575, the French ambassador reported that Elizabeth had killed six deer on a single hunt.

Elizabeth was one of the best-educated women in England. She spoke six languages and mastered the lute (right) and the virginal, a harpsichord-like instrument.

Elizabeth turned down many marriage proposals from European kings and nobles and stayed childless throughout her life. Perhaps she feared that she would lose power to a husband or that England would be drawn into war if she married a foreigner. Some think that she was influenced by her mother's execution on the orders of her father. Instead, she lavished titles and fortunes on a number of court favorites who served her loyally for their entire lives. Under Elizabeth's rule, England was a Protestant country. The Church of England became fully established. Catholics were not officially outlawed and were mostly safe from persecution. This angered both Protestant and Catholic extremists, and Elizabeth came under threat from a string of plots. In 1568, Elizabeth's cousin, Mary, Queen of Scots, fled Scotland to seek refuge at Elizabeth's court. Catholic rebels plotted to unseat Elizabeth and place Mary on the English throne. Mary was charged with treason and then beheaded in 1587.

The queen was a skilled rider who loved to gallop at high speeds, often with Robert Dudley, one of her closest favorites at court.

Elizabeth performs the volta dance, popular during the 1500s. The queen had a great love of music, poetry, and plays, which all flourished during her reign.

Mary, Queen of Scots, was kept prisoner in England for 18 years. After a plot to murder Queen Elizabeth was uncovered in 1586, Mary was found guilty of involvement and was executed.

Sir Francis Walsingham (left) was Elizabeth's royal secretary. He built up a network of spies that helped uncover many plots to remove the queen from power.

After an early failure to capture part of France, Elizabeth avoided costly wars. Instead, she encouraged piracy and played rival nations against one another. She sent aid to Protestants who were fighting the Spanish in France and, in 1585, the Netherlands.

Twenty-five years earlier, the Spanish king, Philip II, had offered to marry Elizabeth. Now he turned hostile, angered by the execution of his fellow Catholic ruler, Mary, Queen of Scots. In 1588, across the narrow stretch of water separating England from Europe, Philip amassed a huge invasion force of around 130 ships— the Spanish Armada. With a further 30,000 soldiers on land, the situation looked bleak for England.

Elizabeth knights Francis Drake in 1581. Drake was one of several English sea captains who were encouraged to raid other countries' colonies and to plunder their treasure ships.

Despite the outlook, fortune favored the English from the start. Various incidents delayed the Armada before it could set sail. The experienced admiral, Marqués de Santa Cruz, died, and his replacement had little naval experience. The ponderous Spanish galleons, ideal for the calm waters of the Mediterranean Sea, were less suited to the choppy North Sea and English Channel.

For one week, the lighter English vessels harassed the Spanish, launching hit-and-run cannon attacks along the south coast of England. The Spanish ships sailed to France, where they were defeated in Gravelines. Storms and heavy winds forced the Armada to retreat north around Scotland and Ireland, where the rocky, treacherous coasts took their toll. Less than 70 ships made it back to Spain, many of them battered beyond repair. Although poor planning and bad weather had inflicted a lot of the damage, Elizabeth seized the opportunity to claim a glorious victory and the respect of England's European neighbors.

Shortly before the Armada's attack, Elizabeth rallied her troops with a rousing speech in which she said she had the stomach and heart of a king.

The English sailed fire ships into the Spanish Armada, moored in Calais. In panic, the Spanish raised anchor to avoid the blazing vessels.

Elizabeth is carried through one of the towns of her kingdom. She shrewdly built an image as the Virgin Queen or Good Queen Bess, married to her country and serving its people loyally.

At home, Elizabeth took great care over her image, and her public outings were stage-managed to look as grand as possible. In later life, however, the queen was far from beautiful. Half bald and scarred by a near-fatal bout of smallpox, she was forced to wear wigs and heavy makeup. Still, she attracted the attentions of new court favorites. The last of these, Robert Devereux, turned against her and mounted a feeble rebellion that was easily crushed.

The question of who would succeed Elizabeth had taxed her government for many years. By the time she fell ill and died at Richmond Palace in 1603, secret negotiations had already established that James VI of Scotland—the son of Mary, Queen of Scots—would be crowned James I of England. It was the end not only of the Tudor era of English history but also the life and reign of one of Great Britain's most fascinating rulers.

LIFE LINK
Elizabeth I sent aid to Henry of Navarre (later Henry IV of France) during the French Wars of Religion. Henry was a Huguenot (French Protestant). One of his grandsons became Elizabeth I's successor, James I. Another grandson was King Louis XIV of France.

Louis XIV

February 1651. Twelve-year-old Louis XIV lay in bed, his heart pounding. The baying of the crowd below his bedroom in Paris grew louder and louder. Demanding to see their young king, they began to smash down the palace gates . . .

Louis's childhood had been difficult ever since his father died when he was almost five. A major revolt broke out in 1648, forcing Louis and his mother, Anne of Austria, to flee from Paris on several occasions. Anne was plotting another escape that same night in 1651, but the angry mob forced a change of plan. They were let in to see Louis, crowding around until they were satisfied that their young king had not taken flight from the palace.

When the crowd of Parisians burst into the bedroom, Louis pretended to be fast asleep.

As a young king in his teens, Louis was happy to let Cardinal Mazarin rule France as the regent, a type of coruler.

Louis's birth had been greeted with great joy and surprise throughout France because his parents had been married for 23 childless years. He was named Louis Dieudonné, meaning "Louis, gift from God." After the death of Louis's father, Cardinal Jules Mazarin took power. He ended several wars and crushed the five-year revolt in 1653. Peace with Spain was finally secured when Louis married the king of Spain's daughter, Maria Theresa, in 1660.

Louis examines a rich tapestry. Many new industries, such as silk and glassmaking, were established during his reign.

After Mazarin's death in 1661, Louis shocked France by declaring that, instead of relying on a first minister to run the country, he would take total control. He stamped his authority on the country from the start. He sent the minister of finance, Nicolas Fouquet, to prison and replaced him with Jean Baptiste Colbert. France was a powerful nation of 18 million people, the largest in Europe. To win the fame and glory he craved, Louis needed a firm grip on his subjects. Many French people had grown tired of Mazarin and the nobles, who had gotten rich from unfair and heavy taxes. Colbert reorganized taxes and brought the nobles under control by insisting that they attend Louis's court.

Many French city dwellers and peasants had been thrown into poverty and squalor by years of high taxes and the damaging rebellion known as the *fronde* (1648–1653).

Louis's minister of war, Marquis de Louvois, built up France's army so that at its peak it numbered more than 400,000 troops. In 1667, Louis attacked Spanish territories to the east of France, winning land and fortresses. This was followed by an invasion of the Netherlands in 1672. When peace was declared six years later, France had gained many towns and a lot of land.

Life at King Louis's court was very ordered and rigid. A gentleman had to sit down in a certain way . . .

. . . a lady had to place her hand on top of a gentleman's bent arm as they strolled through the palace . . .

. . . and a courtier who wanted to speak to Louis had to scratch on the king's door with his little finger.

After Louis danced in a ballet as the sun god Apollo, he became known as the Sun King. It was said that all of France revolved around him.

The extravagant palace of Versailles took about 36,000 workers to construct. The grounds contained 400 sculptures, a canal, and even a smaller palace called the Grand Trianon.

Louis made plans to move his court away from Paris, partly to lessen the power of certain nobles. In the 1660s, work began on transforming a hunting lodge in Versailles into the grandest palace in the world. The royal family finally took up residence in 1682.

Versailles was a place of true wonder to everyone in Europe. Everything about the palace was astonishing—from the 37,000 acres of gardens and enormous stables that could hold 12,000 horses to its 1,400 fountains and the Opera, an opulent room that was lit by 10,000 candles.

Europe's most wealthy, powerful, and creative people craved an invitation to Versailles. There they saw the king lead a life of great pomp and ceremony. Louis had other homes, too, such as the chateau of Marly, where he lived much more simply.

Under Louis, France became the cultural center of Europe. He set up academies for painting and sculpture, science, architecture, and music.

Many great artists flocked to Versailles, from the playwright Molière to the painter Charles Lebrun, and French became the most fashionable language in Europe. Louis himself was nicknamed the Sun King. His glittering rule would inspire many other kings and queens, including Russia's Catherine the Great and Frederick the Great of Prussia.

Away from their power bases, French nobles jostled for favor at Louis's court. The ultimate honor was to guide the king to his bedchamber at night.

Louis strides through the magnificent Hall of Mirrors, decorated with giant chandeliers and more than 300 mirrors.

In 1682, René de la Salle claimed most of the land around North America's Mississippi River for France. He named it *La Louisiane* in honor of his king.

The Man in the Iron Mask was a famous prisoner during Louis's reign. His true identity remains a mystery to this day.

France suffered its first major defeat for 50 years at the savage Battle of Blenheim in Bavaria. English and Austrian forces (right) killed thousands of French troops.

The year 1683 was a turning point in Louis's life. Both his chief minister, Colbert, and his wife died, and the king made some rash decisions. From 1685, he began to persecute the Huguenots, France's main group of Protestants. Around 200,000 Huguenots fled to England and elsewhere, taking with them large amounts of money and their valuable business and industrial skills.

The Protestant powers of Europe, such as England, the Netherlands, Denmark, and Austria, were alarmed by France's growing power and its persecution of the Huguenots. They formed the League of Augsburg and raised arms against France in the Nine Years' War (1688–1697). Battles broke out in the Spanish Netherlands and as far away as North America and the Caribbean. Louis forced farmers to join his army, and the French people suffered famines, food shortages, and other hardships.

By the time a peace treaty was signed, all sides were exhausted and running out of money. Louis had to give back much of the territory he had won, but peace did not last long. War broke out again in 1701, and Louis suffered devastating defeats at the hands of the English and other armies in Blenheim (1704) and Ramillies (1706). A stalemate was reached but at a huge cost to France. In 1715, Louis died. His 72-year reign was the longest that Europe had ever seen. Many people were relieved at the Sun King's death— his costly wars and lavish spending had almost bankrupted France. Yet Louis XIV also left his country greatly changed, with powerful authorities and a vibrant culture that dominated Europe long after his death.

On his deathbed, Louis gave advice to his successor and great-grandson, Louis XV.

LIFE LINK
Louis XIV once refused to allow Prince Eugene of Savoy to join the French army. Years later, Frederick the Great, a young Prussian prince at the time, served under Eugene, who had become one of Europe's greatest generals.

Frederick the Great

November 1730. Guards burst into a cell in the fortress of Küstrin and wakened its prisoner at 5 A.M. Frederick, the heir to the throne of Prussia, had been held in solitary confinement for many days. Tired of his father's bullying, he had been captured trying to flee to England with his friend Hans Hermann von Katte.

The 18-year-old prince was dragged to the window and forced to watch a terrible scene. In the courtyard below stood von Katte, who waved cheerfully and smiled. Moments later, Frederick's friend was dead, beheaded by a saber on the orders of Frederick's father, Frederick William I, the king of Prussia.

Frederick is held by a guard, about to witness the execution of his close friend von Katte. Moments later, the prince fainted.

Frederick was trained to march like an army officer by the age of five. He was woken early each day by a cannon shot and given a full-size military drum to beat.

When the king (far right) first saw Frederick after the escape attempt, he drew his sword in fury. The prince's life was saved by General Wilhelm von Buddenbrock, who threw himself between the two.

Frederick's father was a practical military man. His palace in Potsdam near Berlin was plain compared to others in Europe. He bullied his wife and children and thought nothing of ridiculing Frederick in public or striking him with his cane. He loathed his eldest son's love of reading and painting and once beat him for hiding in some shrubs to read a book rather than going on a deer hunt.

Frederick's escape attempt set off a chain of violent events ordered by his father. Some of his army colleagues were sent to Spandau Prison, a young musician friend was publicly whipped, and his sister—called "the scum, Wilhemina" by their father—was threatened with the death penalty.

Frederick escaped execution but was forced to stay in Küstrin to work as a lowly civil servant.

On the orders of his father, Frederick married Elizabeth Christine, the daughter of a German nobleman, in June 1733.

Relations with his father thawed a little after Frederick's marriage. In 1734, he was allowed back into the army. He studied the tactics of the famous general Eugene of Savoy. One year later, he was sent to East Prussia, where his military duties took up little time. At Rheinsberg Castle, Frederick read voraciously, studied politics and warfare, and discussed intellectual matters. He also exchanged letters with the famous French philosopher Voltaire, whom he admired greatly.

Following his father's death in 1740, Frederick was crowned king of Prussia. Almost at once he led his country into war. The army was well trained, but Prussia was still only a minor power with scattered territories. Frederick's first target was Austrian-controlled Silesia (now part of Poland), a province of rich farmland, textile factories, and mines. His forces overtook the region, but Austria fought back, dragging France and other European nations into battle. Frederick's aggressive tactics and his fast, lightly armed cavalry turned the war in his favor. Prussia won East Friesland and Silesia to become the fifth major power in Europe after France, Great Britain, Russia, and Austria.

In 1741, Frederick fled the Battle of Mollwitz when it appeared lost to Austria. Prussian soldiers galloped after the king to announce their victory.

The Bayreuth Dragoons were part of Frederick's formidable cavalry. They were the key to victory at the Battle of Hohenfriedberg, when Prussian troops killed around 7,000 Austrians and took 6,000 prisoners.

Frederick threw himself into the task of modernizing Prussia. The king himself would oversee almost any policy, from training troops and draining marshes for new farmland to rewriting Prussia's laws. He ordered the building of a Baltic seaport, Swinemuende, and canals to join the waterways of Berlin to the Oder and Elbe rivers. In the 1760s and 1770s, he encouraged people to move to isolated parts of Prussia with the promise of free wood, animals, and seeds. He also boosted his country's industry by investing in factories and opening dozens of coal mines. New laws banned people from importing goods from other countries that could be made in Prussia.

Early in his reign, Frederick banned the use of torture on Prussian citizens.

Frederick hatched a cunning plan to encourage potato farming. His own royal potato field was heavily guarded, which made locals think that the plants were worth stealing for their own fields.

Austria, however, had not forgotten its humiliation over Silesia. By the mid-1750s, a formidable group of powers, including Austria, France, Russia, Sweden, and Saxony, were threatening to attack Prussia. In August 1756, Frederick decided to strike first— he invaded Saxony. The Seven Years' War that followed (1756–1763) would turn into a battle for Prussia's own survival.

Voltaire (right) stayed at Frederick's court for three years. They started to argue, however, and Voltaire was arrested by Frederick's soldiers.

Success came fast for Prussia. Two of Frederick's finest victories were at the Battle of Rossbach and against the Austrian army in Leuthen in 1757. But the overwhelming number of troops in the armies against him took their toll. Frederick's forces suffered a heavy defeat in Hochkirch in 1758 and devastation by the Russians in Kunersdorf one year later.

Prussia's armies and resources were dwindling fast. Russian forces invaded Berlin briefly in 1760, France captured Marburg, and Sweden and Russia occupied parts of Pomerania. All looked lost until the leader of Russia, Elizabeth, died suddenly in 1762. Her successor, Peter III, was a great admirer of Frederick, so he withdrew from the war. Without the support of Russia, the Austrians were repelled at the battle of Freiburg and Prussia held onto Silesia. It had survived against the combined strength of three of Europe's largest powers.

Frederick built an uneasy alliance with Peter III's successor, Catherine the Great. When Prussia, Russia, and Austria divided up Poland in 1772, Frederick gained vital territory that linked East Prussia to the center of his kingdom. Although Prussia never became the cultural center of Europe, as Frederick had hoped, its borders were now secure.

King Frederick was a talented musician who composed more than 100 sonatas for the flute, which he would sometimes play at court.

Frederick surveys the two sides before the Battle of Rossbach. He often led his troops into battle, and it was said that six horses were shot away from under him.

In Rossbach, 21,000 Prussians (in blue) faced twice as many Austrian and French troops. Using stealth, speed, and decoy moves, the Prussians beat their opponents.

In contrast to his military success, Frederick's personal life ebbed away. He never grew close to his wife, and his influential sister, Wilhemina, died in 1758. The king died childless, so the crown passed to his nephew, Frederick William II.

Frederick the Great's legacy is difficult to judge. He expanded his country's territory and worked hard to build a fair, well-run nation that was tolerant of different religions. Frederick saw himself as "the first servant of the state," but his aggressive military tactics would later inspire dictators such as Napoleon and Adolf Hitler.

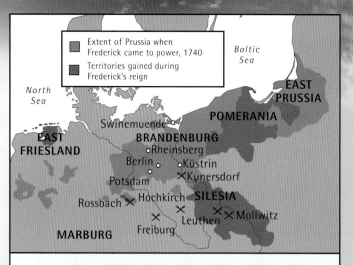

Legend:
- Extent of Prussia when Frederick came to power, 1740
- Territories gained during Frederick's reign

North Sea · Baltic Sea · EAST PRUSSIA · POMERANIA · EAST FRIESLAND · BRANDENBURG · Swinemuende · Rheinsberg · Berlin · Küstrin · Potsdam · ×Kunersdorf · Rossbach× · ×Hochkirch · SILESIA · ×Leuthen · ××Mollwitz · MARBURG · ×Freiburg

Growth of Prussia under Frederick the Great, 1740–1786

The elderly king led a lonely life, preferring the company of his greyhounds to people. He had only one set of simple clothes and his battle-worn military uniforms.

LIFE LINK
Frederick helped arrange the marriage of Sophie Friederike Auguste von Anhalt-Zerbst to the heir of the Russian throne. Sophie went on to become Catherine the Great, the ruler of Russia. She made alliances with Frederick, writing him more than 180 letters.

Catherine the Great

New Year's Day 1744. The family of 14-year-old Sophie Friederike Auguste von Anhalt-Zerbst received an extraordinary letter. Sophie was summoned to Moscow by the formidable Czarina Elizabeth, the ruler of Russia and the most powerful woman in Europe. Within two weeks, Sophie had left her home 60 mi. (100km) southwest of Berlin, accompanied by her headstrong mother, Johanna, and a carriage full of servants. Ahead of her was a 40-day, 1,120-mi. (1,800-km)-long journey into the unknown.

Sophie was born into a minor German noble family that lived in Szczecin (Stettin), a dreary port on the Baltic coast. Her father served in the Prussian army and her mother was an ambitious noblewoman. She scolded and sometimes beat Sophie, showed her little love, and was more interested in plotting her family's rise away from Szczecin and into royal circles.

At the age of seven, Sophie's spine was left deformed by pneumonia, fever, and possibly rickets. Szczecin's hangman suggested that she wear a wooden corset day and night for 18 months, and slowly her spine straightened.

Sophie's journey from Szczecin to Moscow was cold and arduous. Her mother was hurt in an accident, and by the time they reached Russia, Sophie's feet were so swollen that she had to be carried.

Sophie flung herself into life at the Russian court. She went to a masked ball with Peter, made great efforts to please everyone she met, and began to learn the Russian language.

Sophie was 13 when, in November 1742, her father became the ruler of the tiny principality of Anhalt-Zerbst. That same month, far away in Russia, the nephew of Czarina Elizabeth, Karl Peter Ulrich, became Grand Duke Peter and the heir to the Russian throne. Elizabeth knew Sophie's family well—she had once planned to marry Sophie's uncle Karl. When Elizabeth was crowned Russia's ruler, Sophie's mother spotted the glimmer of opportunity and wrote gushing letters of praise to the czarina.

Sophie and Johanna arrived in Moscow in time for Grand Duke Peter's lavish 16th birthday party. Sophie soon realized that the czarina was considering her as a wife to the grand duke. She worked hard to win the czarina's affection. The following year, Sophie married Peter, having taken a new Russian name—Yekaterina, or Catherine.

Catherine married Peter after converting to the Russian Orthodox religion. Shortly afterward, her mother was sent back to Prussia by Czarina Elizabeth. Catherine never saw her parents again.

Catherine enjoyed a fairy-tale wedding, although her marriage to Peter was anything but happily ever after. Sharing almost nothing in common, the pair often bickered, and the princess soon grew wary of the many spies and intrigues that plagued the Russian court.

During the coup to overthrow Peter, Catherine marched at the front of more than 10,000 loyal soldiers.

In 1761, Czarina Elizabeth died and Peter was crowned Czar Peter III. To great anger, he withdrew from a war against Prussia, a country that he admired very much, and tried to impose Prussian ways on his people. Gossip spread that he would divorce Catherine and marry his mistress, Elizabeth Vorontsova. Catherine had affairs, too, including one with Gregory Orlov, a soldier. Orlov and his brother Aleksey, along with other nobles and army officers, plotted a coup to seize power in 1762. Peter was dethroned and then murdered, and Catherine declared herself the czarina. Rumors of Catherine's role in her husband's death swept across Europe, although, to this day, no one knows whether or not she was involved.

Peter was a childish man who loved to play with toy soldiers and puppet shows. It is said that he court-martialed and executed a rat for eating two of his toys.

When Catherine was stopped from seeing her newborn son, Paul, in 1754, she clashed with the czarina. Catherine was not close to Paul and made sure that he was never a threat to her reign.

One week after Peter had been forced to abdicate as the czar, he was murdered by unknown attackers.

Few Russians gave the newly crowned Catherine II a chance—she was a minor German princess with no direct claim to the throne. But they underestimated this czarina's intelligence. She had lived in Russia for almost 20 years and had studied its people and politics closely.

During her first years in power, Catherine raised money by claiming back property from the church. She brought in new farming, mining, and steel-making techniques from overseas and increased trade with other nations. She opened schools and hospitals and demanded that her governors throughout Russia send back accurate maps, crop reports, and population counts.

In September 1762, Catherine was crowned the czarina in Moscow. She took control of her adopted country with great energy, shocked at the backwardness of Russia's laws and by how empty its treasury had become.

To become a great power, Russia needed ports on the Baltic and Black seas. Catherine began to expand her country's territory and influence. She was involved in the division of Poland, which gave Russia access to the Baltic coastline, and fought off the armies of her cousin Gustav III of Sweden in 1790. And by triumphing over the Ottoman Empire in two long, bitter wars (1768–1774 and 1787–1792), Russia won ports on the Black Sea, as well as vast new territories such as Ukraine and Crimea.

But in 1773, Yemelyan Pugachev, a Cossack soldier wounded in the first Ottoman war, launched a rebellion. Life in wartime Russia was harsh and became more difficult as a plague swept through the country. Pugachev organized an army of unhappy peasants, soldiers, and workers, but when they began to truly threaten Catherine, she sent a strong force to defeat the rebels.

The rebel Pugachev was captured by his own defeated soldiers, taken to Moscow in a metal cage, and then tried and beheaded in 1775.

Catherine never remarried after Peter's death, but she placed many of her former lovers, including Grigori Potemkin (above), in positions of great power.

At the Battle of Chesma in 1770, Aleksey Orlov crushed the Ottoman navy. On the same day, Russian troops won a land battle in Larga, turning the tide of war in their favor.

Growth of the western Russian Empire during Catherine's reign, 1762-1796

After the uprising, Catherine began to encourage serfdom—the medieval system under which millions of Russians were treated almost as slaves, forced to work the lands of wealthy nobles. She modernized Russia and built new industries, but few rural peasants felt the benefits of her reforms. Nobles, merchants, and intellectuals most enjoyed the flourishing of the nation as Catherine promoted arts and culture like no Russian ruler had ever done before.

Catherine had to fight off threats to her crown from Princess Tarakanova—who claimed to be Czarina Elizabeth's daughter—and a former czar, Ivan VI, who had been an infant when Elizabeth took power. Her reign finally came to an end when she died in 1796. She had survived in a man's world as the head of a nation that was foreign to her and had built on the achievements of earlier Russian rulers, such as Peter the Great, to modernize Russia and extend its empire.

In 1768, Catherine invited a British doctor, Thomas Dimsdale, to Russia. He advised how to fight smallpox and inoculated the czarina against the disease.

In 1787, to celebrate 25 years in power, Catherine toured her newly won lands in Crimea. The lavish party set out in 124 sleighs and 30 large coaches.

Other famous kings and queens

William the Conqueror (1027–1087)

In September 1066, William, the duke of Normandy in northern France, gathered a large army of Normans and crossed the English Channel. The following month, he defeated Harold Godwinson at the Battle of Hastings. He marched to London to be crowned King William I of England. William reorganized England's government, granted land to the Normans, and ordered a detailed survey of the country's lands, people, and possessions that became known as the Domesday Book. He spent most of the last 15 years of his life in Europe, having established Norman influence over England.

Tamerlane (1336–1405)

Born in Uzbekistan, Tamerlane (also known as Timur the Lame) was the son of a minor chieftain. After fighting for many years to secure power in his own region, he began to conquer nearby lands. In the 1380s, his army, many of whom were archers on horseback, advanced rapidly through Iran, Georgia, Armenia, and into Russia. They marched as far west as Syria and Turkey and also invaded India. Tamerlane was brutal on the battlefield, where he executed thousands of defeated enemies, but he was also a great lover of the arts and built many beautiful palaces in Central Asia.

Peter the Great (1672–1725)

Peter was the first czar to look overseas in order to modernize Russia. He toured Europe and brought back new practices in shipbuilding and other industries. He set up a new capital city in St. Petersburg and established the first regular Russian army and navy. A giant of a man, Peter had inexhaustible energy and a thirst for learning. Yet he could also be cruel—he once ordered the execution of more than 1,000 soldiers on suspicion of plotting against him.

Queen Victoria (1819–1901)

Victoria became the queen of Great Britain in 1837. She had nine children, many of whom married into European royalty, so Victoria became known as the Grandmother of Europe. After the death of her husband, Prince Albert, she disappeared from public life for many years. Victoria had little real power but was an important figure in Great Britain during a century of enormous change. Her 64-year reign was the longest of any previous British king or queen.

Glossary

Abdicate To give up the position of king or queen.

Calligraphy The art of beautiful handwriting.

Catholic A member of the Roman Catholic church, the Christian community led by the pope.

Cavalry An army unit made up of soldiers on horseback.

Conquistador A Spanish conqueror of the civilizations of Central and South America.

Convent A place where nuns live, pray, and work.

Coup A sudden attempt to overthrow a leader, often by force.

Court The place where a king or queen has a household and conducts official business.

Court-martial To put somebody on trial in a military court.

Czar An emperor of Russia.

Depose To remove someone from power.

Dictator A leader who has total control over a country, usually unelected and ruling by force.

Disown To refuse to have anything more to do with something or someone.

Divine right The belief that monarchs receive their authority directly from a god.

Fire ship A ship loaded with explosives, deliberately set on fire and left to drift among an enemy's warships.

First minister The most senior member of a government.

Galleon A large, slow, and sturdy ship used by the Spanish from the 1500s to the 1700s.

Governor A person who runs part of a country.

Import To bring goods from another coutry to sell in your own country.

Infantry An army unit made up of soldiers who fight on foot.

Interrogation The thorough questioning of somebody.

Mercenary A soldier paid by a foreign country to fight in its army.

Mortuary temple A building where dead bodies are kept and preserved before burial.

Mosque A building where Muslims worship.

Muslim A follower of the religion of Islam, which was founded by the prophet Muhammad.

Obelisk A tall pillar with four sides and a pointed top.

Occupy To capture a city or a country.

Pagan A person who follows any pre-Christian religion, especially one with many gods.

Partition Dividing something into smaller parts.

Persecution Unfair treatment, often because of political or religious beliefs.

Philosopher A person who studies the meaning of the universe and human life.

Principality A territory ruled by a prince or a princess.

Propaganda Communicating ideas and information, sometimes using lies or exaggeration, to persuade people to think or act in a certain way.

Protestant A member of the many different Christian churches that separated from the Catholic church in the 1500s.

Province A region of a country.

Reform To try to make something better by changing it.

Reformation A 16th-century religious and political movement that attempted to reform the Catholic church but led to the birth of many Protestant churches.

Regent A person who rules while a monarch is either too young or too ill to govern.

Rickets A disease that softens the bones, usually of children.

Serfdom A system found in medieval Europe in which peasant serfs were forced to work in the fields of landowners.

Smallpox An infectious disease that causes fever and spots.

Solitary confinement Being kept alone in a special prison cell.

Tactician A person who uses carefully prepared tactics (plans) to win a battle or contest.

Territory An area of land that is run by one country or ruler.

Treasury The organization that controls a country's money.

Vizier A high-ranking official in some Muslim countries.

Index